Little Girl
BE HEALED
and HAPPY

Little Girl BE HEALED *and* HAPPY

Thrusting Her Into Her Greatness

NADINE N SLAUGHTER

Xulon Press
555 Winderley Pl, Suite 225
Maitland, FL 32751
407.339.4217
www.xulonpress.com

Xulon PRESS

© 2024 by Nadine N Slaughter

All rights reserved solely by the author. The author guarantees all contents are original and do not infringe upon the legal rights of any other person or work. No part of this book may be reproduced in any form without the permission of the author.

Due to the changing nature of the Internet, if there are any web addresses, links, or URLs included in this manuscript, these may have been altered and may no longer be accessible. The views and opinions shared in this book belong solely to the author and do not necessarily reflect those of the publisher. The publisher therefore disclaims responsibility for the views or opinions expressed within the work.

Paperback ISBN-13: 979-8-86850-168-5
Ebook ISBN-13: 979-8-86850-169-2

Table of Contents

Chapter 1 Life Changing Move 1

Chapter 2 Horror Came Too Soon 7

Chapter 3 Moving To The City 11

Chapter 4 Teenage Crush 19

Chapter 5 Brokenness Reappeared 25

Chapter 6 Time To Be A Responsible Adult 31

Chapter 7 Paternal Grandparent History 37

Chapter 8 Back Slidden 39

My Story

Not every little girl grows up broken; many grow up in a happy and healthy environment, having never been violated. Regrettably, in contemporary society, the occurrence of young girls being subjected to violation has become excessively prevalent. Unfortunately, at a very young age, I was exposed to physical and emotional harm.

For a couple of decades, I have grappled with the emotional torture from the harm I was instilled with as a young girl without healing. Despite various efforts to curb the vice, instances of sexual violation remained prevalent. Many women continue to endure this pain and struggle to find forgiveness for themselves and the individuals responsible for violating them. It is imperative that we grant God, or any other name by which you choose to address the divine, the opportunity to restore and maintain our well-being. As much as we want to be happy, it's not always easy. When we understand that God created us to be free and happy according to His word, we can get through this because He carries us in His hands. It's as though He picks us up and carries us in His arms, giving us comfort and strength by His Holy Spirit.

CHAPTER 1
Life Changing Move

I recall being in the front seat of my grandfather's truck, on my mother's lap, while we relocated from Cassopolis to Niles, Michigan, when I was about four years old. At that time, I believed my mom and dad were going through a divorce, and we were forced to move with just my mother and four other siblings. Although I was unaware that three of my grandparents had passed away at the time, I do recall the presence of my mother's mother. At that time, she was married to my step-grandfather. They were both benevolent individuals, and I recall that they resided in town opposite the cemetery in Niles. We lived out in what was called the country, which was about fifteen minutes away from our grandparents. Shortly after our relocation, my grandmother passed away.

Growing up, I heard many great stories about how sweet and kind she was and how she served at Mount Calvary Baptist Church, which we attended.

People would constantly remind me of how much I resembled her.

After my grandmother passed away, my grandfather remarried a nice lady from Boston. We used to call her Miss Sally, a woman who consistently adorned herself in exquisite, custom-made suits and hats. Grandpa was always dressed very nicely, and she also made suits for him. They would sometimes pick us up on Saturdays and take us to church. We went to their house after church where we ate vegetarian food, played outside, and were then instructed by Miss Sally on how to weed the yard and plant flowers from seeds.

I began ordering seed packets when I was about eight years old, as I just adore watching flowers develop and planting them. I distinctly recall the azaleas, xenias, and marigolds that I cultivated in front of our residence. It gave me such a happy feeling of freedom and excitement when I saw them bloom and blossom. I will never forget how excited I was when my mom helped me order my first three packs of flowers. I repeatedly dashed to the mailbox in anticipation of their arrival, and they eventually did. What a delight! To this day, I still have a deep passion for cultivating flowers.

Miss Sally was an amazing seamstress; she taught me my first two stitches. One was how to hem a dress or pants, and the other stitch was to repair a hole in a seam. She also taught a homemaker class at my middle school. I had a lot of respect for her; she was so kind to my grandfather and us.

At some point, Miss Sally and my grandfather traveled to Paris, where she bought me a beautiful pair of shoes. They were burgundy with a strap up the middle and about a two-inch heel. I absolutely loved those shoes and wore them so proudly for several years. They took another trip to Ohio and brought me a Cincinnati Bengals t-shirt. I didn't know anything about football, but I loved that t-shirt's brown and orange colors. The sight of Bengal's hues brings back fond memories of the joy and gratitude I felt upon receiving that present.

My grandfather owned a car garage where my father used to help him repair cars. I have a picture of him and my grandmother sitting on the side of the truck with "Smitty's Garage" on it. Grandpa told me if I saved up enough money to purchase my first used car, he would match what I had. He informed me of the amount I needed to save and identified a lovely car. I was unsure of the type of car I desired, but I had faith that my grandfather would buy me a nice one.

He kept his word and helped me purchase my first car, a 1970 olive green Fury 3. It was an impeccable car with white wall tires and white leather seats. I was strongly inclined toward tidiness and maintaining a clean personal space from a young age. This habit extended to my car, as I still have an aversion to traveling in a dirty car. I used to wash it by hand and learned over the years how to detail it, which is what I still do to this day. It is a happy and peaceful place for me.

I was captivated by observing my father and grandfather engage in car repairs. I took it upon myself to perform oil changes on my own vehicle, as my father had instructed me in the process. I recall the car having faulty brakes, but thanks to my grandpa's expertise as a mechanic, he installed new brakes on my car. To this day, I wish I could have kept that car.

Years later, Grandpa and Miss Sally moved to Alabama, which was their final resting place. My grandfather passed away first, and we were able to attend his funeral. Unfortunately, a few years later, Miss Sally passed away, and we were unable to attend her funeral.

The road we lived on was not paved, and I have fond memories of strolling down it during the summer with my siblings. We would go across the street and pull down the small trees and bounce up and down on them like they were horses, and we had a blast. In the wintertime on the road, when the snow fell, sometimes the snow ploughs couldn't come down our street, so by the time I was maybe around five years old, we had to walk in the deep snow up to the corner to catch the bus. Mom always ensured that we were warm and wrapped up well; we were happy kids.

Initially, our household accommodated four children; three years later, three more siblings joined us. I don't recall seeing Mom pregnant with these three siblings but remember her mentioning that she was going to have a baby again. I do recall seeing Mom with two different men, not at the same time, other than my father. As a very young child, what I saw and heard still seems so vivid to me.

In my mom's younger years, women were required to be silent. I believe that because of ignorance, they didn't understand the pain and suffering it would cause their little girls, even though it may have happened to them. Most of those behaviors stemmed down generations. From what I have learned from reading the Bible and listening to the Holy Spirit, all the shame and silence were rooted in the spirit of fear. I believe that it was also transmitted to my siblings and myself, as well as to my generation.

CHAPTER 2
Horror Came Too Soon

A few years after moving to that road, I was being fondled by my brothers and two neighborhood boys. I was terrified, ashamed, embarrassed, and at that time, I didn't want to implicate anyone in trouble. I kept this secret to myself for a good twenty years. I at last confided in my older sister about it, as I could no longer suppress my emotions. She said that my brothers and the boys in the neighborhood did not comprehend what they were doing at that age.

Although I valued the sympathy she imparted, I remained broken, feeling like a nasty little girl, and humiliated, just as some of you continue to feel. Please believe that God hasn't forgotten you. He is God Almighty who saves us in my eyes; without His grace and mercy, I would be insane or dead at this very moment.

I am convinced that He dispatched His angels to protect me from every harm, danger, and injury. At that very young age, I felt His presence.

We begin to develop at a very early age, and hormones start playing a part. We begin to feel and experience bodily sensations, and we have no idea what they are. Hormones initiate physiological and psychological changes in our bodies and minds that we were not previously instructed or educated about how to handle. Home is the ideal starting point for early education. However, our parents lacked the knowledge and understanding to convey its importance effectively.

At that age, we begin experiencing physical and emotional sensations that are unfamiliar to us, which arouses our curiosity and prompts us to engage in certain behaviors. Television exposure to adult sexual behavior, including acts of intimacy and kissing, may have influenced our inclination to experiment with such behaviors.

When I was being fondled, I clearly remember feeling a warmness and tickling sensation in my vaginal area. I was horrified and didn't understand what had taken place. I know now that this is the female reproductive system that God created in us. Nevertheless, as a young and naive girl, I was beginning to mature, and I instinctively understood that it was not normal for my brothers or any male to engage in such sexual activities. I finally got enough courage and fight in me to tell them to stop it, and they did. This fleeting period had a limited duration, yet it was sufficient to corrupt the authentic essence of sexuality.

Nevertheless, I experienced fear, shame, and a sense of being alone in such a situation. Back then, I felt like maybe I was doing something to bring this up on myself, as many little girls felt at my age. This was the second dark place that I experienced. I really hate that even women my age still feel this way. It is imperative that we acquire knowledge of the feminine flow in a healthy manner. Little girls, there is so much help for us today, so don't be afraid to reach out. Undoubtedly, God will provide you with an individual or individuals whom you can confide in wholeheartedly, entrusting them with your innermost thoughts and secrets. Simply seek His guidance and attentively listen. Perhaps it may even be me.

I later found out these acts are called incest. Many women are in their sixties and older still carrying this hurt, pain, and shame to this day. They are walking around wounded, manifesting through their behavior of lashing out at one another, their children, and family. They are engaging in the use of derogatory language such as referring to each other as female dogs and other profanities. Some individuals resort to physical violence and, in extreme cases, even commit murder because of the intense anger they harbor within themselves. They haven't forgiven themselves or the person/people that offended them. This is why it is so important for us to know that we are not alone and that our heavenly Father loves us so much. If we give permission to God to restore us, He has the power to not only heal us but also improve us to a state that is twice as good as before.

We must yield our will to Him; we have a choice. As a firsthand observer of this affection, I have understood that I am not to blame for it. I urge all young girls, regardless of their age, to remember that they are not at fault either. I also learned that when someone approaches you, making you feel unsafe, tell them to leave you alone, and if they persist, you are being violated. This may lead to being raped at times, which was another horror that I went through later. Sometimes it even leads to some dying an early death.

CHAPTER 3
Moving to the City

At around age ten, we moved into town. My mom was pregnant with the eighth child. The house only had two bedrooms with a set of bunk beds; my three sisters and I slept in one room, and the three boys slept in the other. Mom would always sleep on a let-out bed in the living room because there was such limited space. She sacrificed so much for us, always ensuring we were good.

Unfortunately, something happened with Mom; it was the first time I had ever witnessed her cry and break down. We later found out that she had discovered that her partner, who she was pregnant with, was having an affair. For some reason, I sensed that her heart was broken, even as a little girl that age. She never really talked to me about what happened. Again, even though I did not comprehend why my mother needed a boyfriend and that they appeared to be kind to us, I felt as though the young girl within me was being separated from my mother by her then-boyfriend, even though he would eventually return her to us.

I remember being sad on occasion, and Mom did take notice and asked me what was wrong. I struggled to express my emotions, but internally, I experienced a sense of isolation and perceived my mother's indifference toward me. When you're just a little girl, you don't really understand anything about your relationship with your parents. Your utmost desire is to witness the happiness of your parents being united, and it deeply saddens you when you observe their separation and divorce, causing immense emotional pain. Again, decades later, God helped me understand that the men my mother dated were fulfilling a need that I never could have. My mother was such a caring person, always looking out for our well-being. I remember asking her why she had so many children, and her reply was that she was the only child. Later, we found out that she had a half-brother.

Within our recently acquired urban residence, there existed a structure commonly referred to as a shed, which served as my personal sanctuary for seeking tranquility and solitude. Interestingly, my brothers and sisters never went into this shed. There were items in the shed that belonged to the owner, and I would just move those things over and make a space for myself. I would build doll houses out of cardboard boxes, make doll clothes, and just be in my own world. It was my happy

MOVING TO THE CITY

place. I always thought I would be a fashion designer at that point.

My cousin Gina would come over, and we'd make doll clothes together because she loved sewing. Gina, who was my very favorite cousin, lived a few minutes away from my house with her parents. I would sometimes walk to her house via the graveyard, which was a shortcut. My grandmother was buried there, and I would go to her grave when I felt lonely. I would sit there and wish I had known her better and even have little talks with her headstone and God about what was happening in my life. I even remember crying sometimes because of the emotional pain that still haunted me from being sexually abused. It gave me a sense of peace when I felt like I couldn't talk to anyone.

My two older and younger brothers got a paper route and asked me if I wanted to help with it. I remember being ten years old in the fifth grade. I would ride on the handlebars and help them throw the papers. My oldest brother would get tip money and say, "Here's something for you for helping me out." We would go to McDonald's, and he would buy me a cheeseburger, then go to the grocery store across the street and buy Hostess chocolate cupcakes with cream on the inside. We had a lot of good times on that paper route. Riding on the handlebars gave me a sense of freedom for some reason; I also felt that my brothers just loved me, and that they truly protected me.

Despite the sexual experiences with them, I now understand that my father's absence had a huge negative effect on my brothers. They also needed his presence to feel protected and guide them. To some extent, I believe my parents did their best with what they learned from their parents, especially considering they married young. I subsequently learned that my father was essentially left to fend for himself, with his aunt and uncle providing minimal assistance.

We just didn't know or understand our father's history. It is evident in retrospect that he merited our compassion, a concept that a child neither comprehends nor is aware of. Back in the day, feelings weren't even discussed, and little boys were told to suck it up. They were told not to cry or even publicly express their feelings. This toxic masculine culture was passed on from the past generation, who arguably were ignorant and mentally enslaved. My heart goes out to grown men who still struggle with not having a space to be vulnerable. I believe that my brothers have father wounds, and I hope that this writing will inspire them to get help and healing.

There was always pain inside of me that I didn't understand or know how to articulate, and I would look sad sometimes. Mom would say, "Nadine, what's wrong?" Because I didn't want her to be sad, I would simply reassure her that everything was fine and say, "Mom, nothing's wrong." I don't really remember her sharing a lot about her childhood. Back then, any young girl at that age didn't really think about asking your parents questions about their childhood, such as "Were you happy when you were a little girl?" or, "Were you ever violated while you were growing up by any men?"

I never genuinely inquired about her relationship with my father or whether he was abusive. I did learn later from my aunt, that my paternal grandfather was physically abusing my grandmother. Auntie stated that she would come home often, seeing her mother with black eyes.

None of the adults I was exposed to talked about their lives. Discourse surrounding that subject was considered taboo; individuals avoided engaging in such discussions or perhaps lacked the vocabulary to express their feelings. Mom occasionally had a boyfriend and would introduce us to them as her friend. They would come and visit for a while or pick her up, but I didn't understand as a little girl.

As I grew older, I understood why I was sad. I thought those men were taking my mom away from me while all they were doing was taking her out on a date. I didn't understand that she also deserved to be hugged, kissed, and made to feel like a woman. She was deserving of feeling exceptional and embodying the invaluable essence of womanhood. She deserved to be a man's priority and needed time away from us to create harmony and balance. As little girls, sometimes we don't understand what we learn along the way. As I started to become a little older, around the age of fourteen, I still felt like both of my parents were rejecting me. Now that I think about it, maybe I was just being territorial without considering that my mother had seven other children to raise. I guess I could call it selfishness.

I can't say that I wasn't happy most of the time because I was. When I went to middle school, I became active in extracurricular activities. I started by singing in the choir at school and really enjoyed singing. Participating in the choir brought me a lot of joy and peace. During my eighth-grade year, I auditioned for the cheerleading squad and successfully secured a spot, marking my inaugural attempt at trying out for any activity.

Mom was proud of me as well. I recall her affirming during my upbringing that I possessed the potential to pursue any vocation or aspiration of my choosing. The cheerleading activity did not sufficiently occupy my time; therefore, I opted to audition for the band and commenced learning to play the French horn.

Despite my lack of proficiency in playing my instrument, I thoroughly enjoyed being a part of the band, particularly the experience of marching. I wanted to make my parents proud of me and feel a sense of satisfaction. At approximately the same time, I commenced work as a library clerk at the Niles Public Library. My mother observed that I exhibited a significant amount

MOVING TO THE CITY

of restlessness due to my constant need for movement. For some reason, I just felt like life had much to offer. I just wanted to experience some of those things. You could say I've felt very entitled at an early age. Even then, being a positive and productive citizen was very important to me. I still hold that high standard today. More importantly, I value showing what God looks like through me.

I began working with my cousin Gina at the Bonanza Steakhouse in Niles. We would go to work in the early morning and work the breakfast shift. At the time, I was around sixteen and could work and go to school for half a day. She was a junior, and I was a senior in high school. Although Gina was my closest cousin, I still couldn't tell her the secret and still didn't want to burden anyone with it. A little girl carrying that burden plays out the scenarios in her mind, thinking about who would believe her. Consequently, I resolved to keep the secret between me and God.

It's amazing what kids can remember at a very early age. I am grateful that, regardless of whether my experiences have been negative or positive, the ability to remember them is a blessing. Were they wounds? Were they painful? Absolutely, yes! But I am still here as an inspiration to little girls going through similar or worse situations. Here, I refer to not only little girls who are young but also little girls who are adults. Sometimes, we think we have had it so bad without understanding that it could be way worse. The experiences I have endured in my life were not as severe or agonizing as those endured by other young girls. This is not a comparison but a reality of what is and what could have been.

CHAPTER 4
Teenage Crush

I had only experienced a teenage crush on one of my cousins' guy friends. I really wasn't interested in getting to know boys, especially in my own hometown. They seemed to be more like homeboys. I really was only focused on school and work. Ultimately, my girlfriend introduced me to one of her out-of-town friends. This young man was very attractive and caught my attention. I felt like he was very street-smart and out of my league but went with the flow. He was way more experienced in dating than me. However, I ended up sleeping with him. He asked me to be his girlfriend and was somewhat aggressive. Again, I really felt violated and ashamed, as if I was looking for love in all the wrong places and feeling that empty void of not having my father around.

I spoke to my mother about wanting to experience having sex and asked if she would take me to get some birth control pills to protect myself from getting pregnant.

I felt that she didn't consider my request seriously and just brushed it aside. At the time, I didn't understand all the things for which she had to be responsible. I am just being honest; as a little girl, I really didn't care. She had seven other children that she was raising as a single parent. I was crying out for help just like some of you were and still are.

Well, the inevitable happened, and I became pregnant. I didn't mention it to my mother and thought I would just hide it. A few months later, she noticed that I had started to grow in my belly area and suggested that I take a pregnancy test. The pregnancy test came out positive, and all I could think about was how I didn't want to bring a child into my mother's home. Yes, I felt the movement of this innocent life inside of me; I felt very afraid, lonely, and embarrassed, not only for myself but also for my mother. I felt like I had let her and my entire family down. I did not tell my father, who was somewhere around. Without hesitation, I contacted the young man and informed him. As expected, he was also scared but thought playing basketball was more important, and being a father was not part of his plan.

My mother asked me what I wanted to do about it, so I chose to abort the baby. That happened two weeks before I graduated from high school. One of my good girlfriends came to visit and check on me. To this day, I will always be grateful for her and others' compassion. I don't recall the conversations I had with my siblings or, for that matter, the young man's parents at that time. Years later, his mother told me that she would have kept the baby. I was curious to know how my mother felt about it. She kept her sadness to herself, but she told me that the child was also a part of her.

Even after this experience, I felt the movement of that innocent unborn child, and I carried the shame and pain around for years until I later learned from reading the Bible and hearing the Holy Spirit telling me that I was forgiven and would see my beautiful baby in Heaven later. Yes, I still wonder what gender the baby was, who it would have resembled and grown up to be, etc. But God, I say, but God. Little girls, we are still alive for the most part, and God has given us a spirit that keeps us strong and a will to want to fight for an amazing life. We want to grow up and be that awesome woman who is successful in all aspects of life. We need connections in our lives to help us get there. I thank God that there were no people in my life who would tell me I would be a failure. I believe a lot of the pain that we as little girls suffer is from people who are not healed and speak to us from a wounded spirit.

Right after high school, I decided to take a correspondence class to be an airline stewardess. That desire stemmed from watching television commercials for stewardesses, as they were then known back in the day, and now they are our flight attendants. I thought they were just so nice, and I wanted to put on that professional image I saw. Something about flying in the friendly skies piqued my interest. I completed several chapters and remembered mailing them to the correspondence school to get them graded, but I quickly got bored because of my energy level, and I quit.

Not only did I have a lot of energy, but I also had a lot of drive and determination to be someone important in society. Mom always told us that we could be anything that we wanted it to be, and I thank God for that. I'd have to say that came from my mother's happiness and, more importantly, her faith in God. We all have a choice of whether to believe in God. I undoubtedly know that believing in God, knowing who He is, and accepting Him in my heart has worked for me. I'm convinced that He never fails to show up through me, as many people confirm this by saying how I always seem to be happy. I just let them know where it comes from and that it's important for me to let that light shine. I truly believe this world wouldn't be so chaotic today if more people would just give Him a chance. By choosing to work after graduating from high school, I knew staying busy doing positive things was important. I saw my mother struggle financially and knew that she deserved better. I don't really remember hearing her complain about taking care of us.

I remember Mom listening to some good music and how she would walk around the house dancing, singing, and smiling in her red lipstick. It seems like I was born

TEENAGE CRUSH

to dance, as even at a young age, people would ask me to dance. I noticed they seemed very happy when they saw me dance, which made me even happier. Mom allowed us to have house parties, as she always wanted to see us happy. She was a wonderful mother in the neighborhood, and the children adored and respected her.

Her joy and laughter, as well as her peace and perseverance, were undoubtedly inspired by God's love in her heart. All of that transitioned over to us. I fully understand that how one is raised has a lot to do with how they grow up. However, we cannot allow the negative things to shape our future. The choices I made to be a good citizen came from within, and I can honestly say that is because we were raised in church. No matter how late we worked or partied, we were still required to attend church. Growing up, Mom would keep Dad updated on how we were doing, and no matter where he was, if he got a bad report about us, he would show up. I believe my father really loved us and supported us the best he knew how. All we can do is see the best in people.

I worked several jobs and took a mobile bus to and from work until I was seventeen years old, which is when I got my first car. At that point, some girlfriends and I would frequent clubs while still maintaining our work commitments. We started to go out of town to Gary and Chicago to different clubs to party. By that time, I had started drinking alcohol and would become intoxicated. But by the grace of God, I'd return home safe. I now realize alcoholism is a family curse in my family. I simply thought I could just numb the pain from my past by drinking.

CHAPTER 5
Brokenness Reappeared

By this time, I do recall two instances when I overdrunk and was taken advantage of. In one situation, I was confined in a boy's house, and he attempted to rape me. My girlfriend and I had offered him a ride home when he invited us to come in. We chatted for a little while before my girlfriend decided she wanted to go to the car. Just after my girlfriend had left, he got aggressive and said that he was going to have sex with me. As we struggled, he carried me up the stairs; all I could do was pray. I cried out to God for help. I remember using the key in my hand to scratch him on his forehead. At that point, he got furious, pushed me down the stairs, and made me sit on the couch.

Across from the couch was his mother's bedroom, where he went under the mattress to reach for something. I remember praying to God that he didn't have a gun to shoot me. So, I ran up to the picture window and began banging on it; at that point, he told me to leave his house as he didn't want his mother's front window broken. Upon leaving his house, I immediately shared with my girlfriend what had transpired; we then went to the police station to record a report. I was outraged, hurt, and disappointed that he would do such a thing, but he wasn't going to get away with it. I still go out and have a good time, even at the club where I met him. I saw him there a time or two, and he once threatened to kill me. Regardless of this encounter, I was still unafraid of this man, and I shared with a few of my guy friends who knew him what he did and told me. They told me not to worry that they would protect me. It wasn't long before I discovered that he was wanted for sexually assaulting other women. Again, this was another addition to more brokenness. However, the bigger girl in me knew it wasn't my fault.

In a second encounter, as I was drunk, another mature guy who had offered me a ride home made me perform oral sex on him in his car. He took advantage of me because he knew that I was drunk. This encounter left me feeling so violated, nasty, and filthy. When you're young and inexperienced, without your father around to protect you, keeping things a secret feels like the only option. It's easy to feel ashamed and like it is your fault. I always knew that saying no to sex was a violation. Yes, at times, I did experience moments of loneliness when all I desired was to be embraced without needing a deep connection. When you're young, lack understanding about your body, and there's no protective presence from your father or brothers, you often find yourself simply going with the flow. Young men say nice things to you to persuade you to do what they want, which still leaves us alone and inexperienced. Again, the little girl is broken.

I was still wounded and not healed or happy, and it's not always a little girl at a particular age; it can be a little girl at any age, even in their fifties and sixties and sometimes until they are even one hundred years old. It seems like we're never totally healed because we're reminded by the Enemy in our minds that we're still in that place. This is when it's so important to affirm who you are and who God sees you as, as well as to remind yourself that you are loved. Continue to remind yourself that you are amazing and beautiful and that you aren't still the wounded, broken little girl. I can't get through each day without asking God to help me remember how He sees me.

The horrible part about both situations was that these two very handsome young men didn't need to force themselves on me. I thought that I really didn't deserve to be violated by them. At that age, I knew they still had no power over me. For some reason, I remained determined to enjoy my life. I've always known that God would protect me and deal with those who mistreated or violated me. I later learned that both young men passed away.

LITTLE GIRL BE HEALED AND HAPPY

Of course, there were older women my mother's age who seemed to have it all together, but we never had deep conversations. We never had conversations about their childhood and how they grew up; they appeared to be put together physically with their makeup, hair, and how they dressed. But only God knows what was really going on in their hearts. I have always admired those women and just wanted to be around them. I think it was because I didn't have my grandmother around. Deep within me, I yearned to inquire about the essence of womanhood, seeking guidance on earning respect in the eyes of a man. It was just that back then at that age, we didn't know what questions to ask. Yes, we were curious. However, we didn't want to overstep our boundaries and ask questions that were too embarrassing, even for them to answer.

When your father is not present and you are young and inexperienced, you do not feel you have anyone to protect you. You keep these secrets because you are ashamed and afraid and believe it is your fault, which it is not. I was always aware that if I said no and a man continued to violate me, it was rape. Yes, I did feel lonely, and all I wanted was to be held and cuddled.

Little girls need to be shown affection by our fathers. Then, when they leave us, we feel so rejected, and sometimes even feel like it was our fault that they left. When we have older brothers around, we trust they will keep us safe, but that's not always the case, especially when they have been broken because their father left them without guidance and without them feeling loved. They, too, carry that pain around for years and take that hurt into their relationships. So many little girls are deeply broken and wounded, and the sad thing is that there is no age limit.

However, if you read my book, just know that God is waiting for you to open your heart and receive His healing power. Just know that it is reasonable and necessary for you to forgive yourself for not knowing any better and that you did your best. Please remember and know that you are okay.

After high school, I continued to work and started dating a young man from Gary, Indiana, that I met at a club where my girlfriend and I used to hang out. We started dating and, of course, sleeping together. I still was not ready to settle down because I was too young. At that age, you have no idea what questions to ask each other or what a committed relationship entails, let alone being monogamous or exclusive. I never intended to be serious with him or even get married. I remember telling him that. We talked a lot on the phone and spent as much time together as possible. I had a car, so I would drive back and forth, picking him up and taking him home.

This back and forth went on for about four years or so while I was being promiscuous with other men. However, I felt he was still connected with his ex-girlfriend, whom he had dated in high school. I didn't understand how a man should show love, or even how to love himself, so that it would make him a good provider or protector. You could say we were just playing house and had no direction. I believe he truly loved me. His parents were still married while my mother was still single. However, while we were dating, Mom got married. His parents did come to our house to meet my parents, but it appears that his mother didn't like me very much. She would tell him that I wasn't allowed to spend the night at the house, but I ended up staying there some nights because driving home late at night wasn't safe.

CHAPTER 6
Time to be a Responsible Adult

As time went on, I decided to go to college. Given that my younger sister was planning to leave, I reasoned that perhaps it would be prudent to pursue the same path to improve my life. Our eldest sister resided in Kalamazoo, the location of the college we aspired to attend, and graciously granted us the use of her residence until our apartment was fully prepared. A few weeks later, we moved in and commenced our new journey.

A few months later, I became pregnant while having an affair with two men: my boyfriend and an older man from South Bend, Indiana. What a mess! I realized that I had once again allowed myself to be ensnared by the words of a man, leading to trouble. I was so ignorant about a committed relationship and staying pure for my future husband. Unfortunately, I didn't know about abstinence or celibacy.

I let both men know that I was pregnant, and either would take full responsibility. My then-boyfriend decided to move in with me and care for me and the baby. At that point, I felt like I needed to get right with God and rededicate my life to Him. I didn't want to live unrighteously while raising this baby. We both went to church, where we learned how to read and study the Word of God with simplicity. For the first time, I liked what I was learning.

My then-boyfriend truly loved me; I could tell. He enrolled in college and got a job to help support me and our daughter. My older sister and the church family gave us a baby shower and gifted us a used baby bed. It was beyond my comprehension how we would survive, but God provided for us by means of family and friends. Unfortunately, the young man and I separated after our daughter turned two years old. I quit school, obtained my own apartment, and began working full-time for a mortgage company. It was the first time I felt a sense of stability with God's help to secure my independence and raise this beautiful little girl.

The little girl in me was still broken, wounded, and traumatized from my past. I found myself being promiscuous again, sleeping with my ex-boyfriend and another man. I became pregnant for the third time and decided to abort the baby. Although I once more felt this innocent life move within me, I refrained from subjecting these two men to the agony of uncertainty. I thought at that time I wanted to save two men's feelings, but I didn't consider my own feelings. It requires both God's forgiveness and our own to be absolved of our errors. I continued to feel as though I had let myself down, but I was compelled to proceed rather than blame myself.

A few years later, I met my future husband at the mailbox where I lived. He moved in with me because I was lonely and felt sorry for him. I didn't know how to live single and whole. I became pregnant for the last time, still while I was sleeping with another man who I was in love with.

Here I went again. I experienced a profound sense of identity confusion and undervaluation in my life. Both men knew that I was pregnant and would take full responsibility. I realize that despite engaging in intimate relationships with men to whom I had no genuine commitment or marital bond, God protected me with exceptional vigilance, as He was aware of His intended plan and purpose for my life. I can say, at least, these men could have made excellent fathers, even though they were in the process of discovering themselves.

My second beautiful baby girl came into the world. I wished that her father was the one I was in love with. The man that I was in love with told me that if it had been his, he would have married me and taken care of us. The day she was born, she looked just like my future husband. I felt so heartbroken and confused and hated myself.

After two years of living together, I began to feel guilty and lost in my thoughts, having no idea who these two lovely baby girls were, much less who I was. As a result, I asked the man I was living with to leave. I had no idea who he was; he seemed like an ordinary person with fatherly wounds. He lashed out, cursed me out, and sat on top of me. I didn't realize that this was domestic violence. Please never feel obligated to tolerate this behavior; if it occurs, seek assistance.

Due to my religious conviction, I resolved to petition God and inquire whether this individual was my spouse. I firmly believed that God had designated this individual as my husband. I was so deceived into thinking that he would change and get better. However, only God can change people as He has changed me; we are all still a work in progress. That's why we need Him; if we were flawless, we wouldn't need God's guidance.

I firmly believed that God had revealed to me that the man was destined to be my husband, which led us to marry three months later. I knew that I was not in love with this man. I perceived him as a potential protector, although he exhibited traits of an irate adult male and could not adequately support me financially. I ignored the red flags and made the mistake of telling him he didn't have to pay rent. I didn't really understand that I was enabling him not to be a responsible grown man.

He had a history of living with other women and not having his own place. When my spiritual mother asked if I was certain I had heard God about marrying the man, I replied, "Yes."

As time went on, the man displayed anger, bitterness, envy, and jealousy, as well as mental and physical abuse toward me. I knew that I didn't deserve such a treatment, but because I was still broken, I didn't have the courage or knowledge to get out. I began experiencing feelings of embarrassment and a diminished sense of self in my roles as a woman, wife, and mother.

I refused to permit my daughters to be brought up in an abusive environment and witness me being subjected to abuse. That was not God's plan for our lives. Children deserve to be brought up in happy and peaceful environments. An attempt to save the marriage through Christian counseling and moving to Georgia failed.

Once again, this piece of writing is not intended to humiliate or criticize men. It is meant to convey valuable life lessons for myself and other women. He was and is a good father to my two daughters, but he was just not a good husband. Although I lacked knowledge on how to be a good wife, I experienced a transformative moment at the wedding ceremony where I was freed from promiscuity and remained faithful for a duration of fourteen years. Following a period of separation lasting two years, the divorce was ultimately finalized.

CHAPTER 7
Paternal Grandparent History

Around this time, my father told me that his mother, who resided in Georgia, was diagnosed with a terminal illness when he was approximately thirteen years old. He explained that their house had been quarantined, and only my grandfather was permitted to reside there to care for my grandmother. On the father's side, there were six siblings in total: two daughters and four sons. My great-grandmother traveled from Michigan and picked up my two aunts and one uncle to take care of them. My paternal great-uncle and aunt, who were Georgia-based, provided care for my father and one brother. My oldest uncle went to serve in the United States Army, I believe.

My dad relocated to Michigan a few years later, where he met my mother. They married soon after and had my eldest sister when they were approximately fifteen and sixteen years old. Within the next four years, they had four other children, whom they called "stairstep children" back in the day. Reflecting on the past, I deeply value the fact that both of my parents chose to have children and dedicated themselves to raising us to the best of their abilities with the assistance of God. I recall Mom telling us that dad used to cut trees to provide for his own well-being and our own. At some point, he had a terrible accident cutting trees where he almost lost his leg.

I can only fathom the psychological toll that must have been on him still yet a teenager, given his marital status and five children. He hadn't reached manhood but was thrusted into the position. Only Dad, Mom, and God truly knew why this marriage did not work out. There are instances when understanding the past of our parents is necessary for both forgiveness and healing to occur.

I can only surmise that my father had confidence in our well-being at that moment, given that my grandmother was still alive. I really want to believe that he had a God-conscious as well. I believe that our fathers are good people, but yes, because of the way they were raised, their fathers lacked direction, wisdom, and revelation. We are such a blessed country here in America, and we have so many resources that there is no reason or excuse to be ignorant. Of course, you must have a desire to learn, grow, thrive, and be the best that God created you to be.

CHAPTER 8
Back Slidden

During a two-year period of separation, I ceased attending church, engaging in prayer, and reading my Bible. I didn't want to see any man and was trying to live happily in my singleness. Subsequently, I began encountering individuals of questionable character, including deceitful and dishonest individuals. Regrettably, I succumbed to temptation, mistakenly believing that I possessed the capability to manage my own life. I began consuming alcohol and operating a vehicle while under its influence, as well as partying in nightclubs.

One day, I experienced two instances where God caused me to have dreams as warnings. The dreams indicated that He was granting mercy by sparing my life, but to fulfill His purpose, I had to cease engaging in sexual immorality.

After making the decision to no longer meet any men, I unexpectedly encountered an exceptional individual.

We had a remarkable relationship characterized by commitment, monogamy, and exclusivity. He showed me what it was to feel adored, admired, respected, pursued, and treated like a real woman. We were planning a life together until he passed away six months later. God had already prepared me for his death in yet another dream.

He spoke to my heart that He allowed me six months to experience true love. He did have a chance to meet my daughters and their fathers, who greatly respected him. Our God will bring you out, little girls.

The fathers of my two daughters have always co-parented. I must give these two men respect for being great fathers to this day. They are believers, and we now have seven amazing grandchildren who mean the world to us.

After studying the Word of God for many years, I learned how to hear God's voice with more clarity. I believe He directed me to live in Georgia for a greater purpose: to meet my father's family and create genealogy, along with building generational wealth. He also led me here to fulfill a dream that He gave me thirty-eight years ago: to become a great transformational speaker, author, and life coach to single women. I will coach married women when I get married for the last time. That dream is the reason I'm writing this book.

He showed me that I was standing at a podium with a long powder blue dress on. I was speaking to the multitudes of a female presence. I couldn't see the ends of the crowd; I still see it clearly today. Over the years, I knew that I was destined to be a speaker. I was uncertain whether it was a teaching or preaching gift, but I did know that I had always enjoyed complimenting young girls and women, an exhorter spiritual gift. My perpetual aspiration is to motivate young girls and women to recognize their intrinsic worth and to complete the magnificent work of creation that God has placed in them.

I recently experienced a very pivotal experience from my youngest daughter. She asked me if I ever sought counseling or therapy to help me navigate through these horrific events. I had only prayed fervently and studied the Word of God until this point.

I am now in therapy with an amazing spirit-filled pastor/psychologist who is making sure I'm good emotionally. For the very first time in my life, my therapist gave me a clear understanding, and I broke down and cried from that hidden pain in the crevices hidden in my heart. I realized I am very selfless and put other's feelings, especially men's feelings, first. I understand that it comes from those daddy daughter wounds. Again, we must continually ask God to remind us how He sees us. It is crucial that we allow the Holy Spirit to lead, guide, and comfort us with His healing power. Doing this will keep your cup full, so to speak.

When you serve people, we must make sure that we are serving ourselves as well, being kind and loving ourselves first. We can bring these things into any relationship. Thanks be to God who causes us to triumph.

LITTLE GIRL BE HEALED AND HAPPY

Little girls of all ages, believe that you are the apple of God's eye and that you don't have to settle for anything less. You are priceless and worthy of being put on a pedestal. Yes, the work all starts with you acknowledging that you may need help and then putting in the action to get and maintain that freedom. Let me inspire you to stay free and be healed and happy, God love you and so do I. Blessings and peace in Abundance.